THE TOKEN ECONOMY SYSTEM

The Instructional Design Library
Volume 19

THE TOKEN ECONOMY SYSTEM

David Lauridsen
Hammond Middle School
Laurel, Maryland

Danny G. Langdon
Series Editor

Educational Technology Publications
Englewood Cliffs, New Jersey 07632

Library of Congress Cataloging in Publication Data

Lauridsen, David.
    The token economy system.

    (The Instructional design library; v. no. 19)
    Bibliography: p.
    1. Rewards and punishments in education.
2. Incentive (Psychology). 3. Performance contracts
in education. I. Title. II. Series.
LB3025.L35   371.5'3   77-25897
ISBN 0-87778-123-0

Printed in the United States of America.

Library of Congress Catalog Card Number:
77-25897.

International Standard Book Number:
0-87778-123-0.

First Printing: February, 1978.

FOREWORD

The Token Economy System instructional design is a well thought out, defined, and workable system for meeting one of our most pressing problems in education—how to change the social behaviors of reluctant learners in a positive direction so that academic learning itself can take place. In this book, David Lauridsen, who has faced and met this problem, will give you the nuts and bolts and not just the blueprint for establishing and maintaining a Token Economy System.

It is fair to say that Token Economy Systems find their most effective and efficient application with reluctant learners. However, it is true that this instructional design has been used for other than reluctant learners and in environments where there is a combination of both reluctant and "cooperative" students. It is also true, as the author points out, that the system can be used to encourage students to learn academic skills as well as to modify in a positive direction their social behaviors. I say this because the author concentrates on reluctant learners and their negative social behavior, out of (1) the desire on his part to concentrate on the most likely circumstances for applying a token economy system, and (2) the limit imposed on him for space in this book within which to describe token economies in general. How this design can concurrently or by itself be used to assist and motivate students to achieve academic skills should be obvious enough. As Series editor, I ask only that you not overlook its use for nonreluctant learners and how it can be applied in learning academic skills.

Finally, this is one of those instructional designs that professional educators tend to get rather emotional about. Any hint that you are going to be "paying the student" for his or her efforts is sometimes seen as "bribery." Since not all humans, including some students, come with an adequate level of built-in self-satisfaction with themselves and what they are doing (or supposed to be doing), other means for enhancing satisfaction can be used until the "self" takes over. They can and do work. The problem isn't usually convincing students; rather, it is convincing some self-satisfied educators who decide what the unsatisfied learner will experience.

Danny G. Langdon
Series Editor

PREFACE

This book was not conceived in an ivory tower or nurtured by high-sounding rhetoric. It is a down-to-earth approach to students who are getting little from their school experience. It provides a learning atmosphere in which good curriculum innovations can "take hold" with previously unresponsive students, and it frees teachers from self-defeating patterns of classroom control. Without apology, it sets out to deliberately and generously reward students for changing their social and academic behaviors.

Far too many programs for reluctant learners fail because the designers are not specific about the behaviors to be changed or the factors which actually control behavior. While they attempt to cultivate growth within the student himself (such as the "enhancement of self-worth"), nothing is done about the contingencies of reinforcement within the school environment which are actually maintaining the behaviors in the first place. Over the last few years, educators have been offered all sorts of elixirs for what ails students. The physical structure of the buildings have been opened, the curriculum revamped for relevance and inquiry, and the teachers "humanized," yet the problems persist. Despite carefully drawn objectives, lessons still fall flat when the students have no incentive to involve themselves. Despite the best intentions of teachers, they still get caught in a seemingly endless cycle of punitiveness just to maintain enough order for a few students to learn something.

Without careful attention to how the reinforcement process works in the school, it is extremely easy to fall into old traps. The author has been there many times. For instance, if a teacher yells at students to stop their misbehavior, and they do, if only temporarily, the teacher is thereby rewarded for yelling—it pays off. The next time around, which will not be long in coming, the teacher is likely to yell again (since rewarded behavior tends to repeat) even if it must now be more forceful and dramatic. Before long, the teacher may be screaming throughout the day without causing anything more than the temporary cessation of undesirable behavior. The trap has been sprung and the students and teacher alike come to dread their captivity. The token economy system offers a way out.

There have been a number of people who have made this program work over the years. As a "token" of my appreciation for their persistence, patience, and professionalism, I wish to acknowledge: Sharon Kasecamp, Mary Lou Skinner, Susan Witty, Kathy Yerep, Eugene Estes, Carolyn Lanier, Hobson Shry, Nancy Chen, Terry Hill, Ron Reis, Albertha Caldwell, Charles Puglisi, Wayne Danley, Elaine Holtzman, and Ellen Reed. Thanks also to Helen McLaughlin for her vigilance at the typewriter.

D.L.

CONTENTS

ABSTRACT

THE TOKEN ECONOMY SYSTEM

This design is intended specifically to help reluctant learners function more effectively in their schools—to change those social and academic behaviors which are prohibiting their own learning and interfering with the learning of others. By creating a highly reinforcing and carefully structured environment, the token economy system permits a variety of instructional approaches to "take hold" with students who previously could not or would not respond to them. In other words, the token system provides the vehicle by which to reach students with new instructional tools.

The design includes procedures for selecting rewards, targeting behaviors, applying reinforcement principles, delivering and exchanging tokens, and evaluating results. The general mechanics of the system are explained in sufficient detail so that they can be readily adopted at the elementary, middle, or secondary level. Not only can the system be applied at all levels, but it can be used in open and closed space arrangements for single or multiple subjects.

THE TOKEN ECONOMY
SYSTEM

I.

USE

This book is intended to serve as a practical guide for implementing a token economy system in the school setting. The system described here provides a comprehensive model of a learning environment which has been carefully structured to meet the needs of students with serious academic and social behavior problems—students who might most aptly be called "reluctant learners." With this alternative program, students who do not function effectively in "regular" school programs, because they seem unable to handle the work, or are unwilling to put forth the effort, or spend the bulk of their time disrupting the learning of others, can be given a structure which makes sense to them and offers real opportunities for success. It is, quite simply, a system which establishes the limits and provides the rewards which are missing from the existing school environment. It is a program which can be readily incorporated into the student's present school without requiring, or even anticipating, the establishment of an alternative school facility.

Teachers, counselors, psychologists, and administrators who are looking for a practical plan of action to help their troubled and unproductive students should find this token economy system sufficiently flexible and inexpensive to serve their purposes. The system can be adapted to the single classroom as well as the open-space pod arrangement. An entire

3

school population can be involved (which is unlikely) or just a specific group of students within the school. This model can be applied to the elementary, middle, and high school levels without necessitating any radical surgery to its basic structure. Perhaps most importantly, this token economy system can be used in all academic subject areas, with "traditional" and "progressive" curricula alike, without losing its potency.

The "point system" (one of the methods covered in this book) has been used successfully for several years in an open-space program involving over 100 middle school students per year, who come into the program with a multiplicity of social and academic problems. The "chip system" (another method to be discussed) has been employed in a variety of closed-space classrooms, for single-subject as well as self-contained instruction. The point system can be used with equal effectiveness in the classroom, but the chip system is impractical for most open-space type programs.

Experience with the system has shown that it is quite workable for both group and individualized instruction. In the model program, for example, the students pass through each day fluctuating between group and individual activities. In the math classes, the students are divided according to skill level into four groups (about 25 students each) within the open-space pod. Simultaneously, one group might be working with Cuisenaire rods, another might be working on learning packets, another might be watching a teacher's chalkboard lesson, and still another might be working in self-pacing booklets. Later in the day, during reading classes, some of the same students might be working in the lab with reading machines, while another group remains in the pod working on functional reading stations.

This particular middle school, which has been the main testing ground for the system, has chosen to bring together under the token economy a group of students who exhibit a wide variety of problems. The instruction is then carefully tailored to meet the students' broad range of academic and social needs. Each year students are selected for the program if they exhibit the following types of behavior problems:

1. Chronic discipline or truancy problems.
2. Learning disabilities or difficulties coupled with inadequate basic skills.
3. Low motivation and serious patterns of underachievement.

By placing this variety of students together under the token economy system, the school has accomplished a number of important goals:

1. To provide a more enjoyable and satisfying environment for the students who have been the most unsuccessful in the past.
2. To substantially increase student motivation and basic skill development.
3. To substantially decrease disruptive and unproductive behaviors.
4. To remove reluctant learners from school programs in which they prohibit other students from learning effectively.
5. To increase the involvement of school specialists and support personnel (reading specialist, learning disabilities teacher, counselor, and aides) with the population who most needs them.
6. To mainstream special education students (specific learning disabled and educable mentally retarded) into a more structured and responsive learning environment.

Many schools may not need a program with such ambitious goals, but this certainly does not preclude them from using all or part of the model token economy system. The basic designs can just as easily be employed in a single class-room or subject area with students who exhibit only one type of learning problem. Regardless of the dimension of the problems in particular schools, the token economy can be the vehicle for providing instruction for reluctant learners. It has been expressly created to deal with the seeming burgeoning number of students who do not relate to present programs and who cannot or should not be simply punished into submission.

The token economy approach recognizes the blunt reality that some students simply do not obtain any personal satisfaction from their school work and are unimpressed by traditional school rewards (grades, promotion, recognition). It further recognizes that many of the discipline problems in today's schools arise from the fact that traditional punishers are no longer potent, for a variety of good and bad reasons. Thus, students who might have previously ("in our day") behaved themselves out of fear of some dire consequences are often no longer threatened by the modern school's arsenal of corrective "weapons." The problems, of course, are often much more complicated than this. But, regardless of how much we argue about the sources of the problems, the hard question remains: What do we do right now with the students who do not seem to care about school, who have no intention of trying, who are unmoved by repeated warnings about their future lives, and who are making the schools difficult, if not impossible, places in which to learn and teach?

The answer seems to reside in how the reinforcement process is harnessed in the school environment. We know from research that most human behavior is shaped and maintained by its consequences, and the school, with its array of rewards and punishers, plays a central role in this process (for better or worse). If the reinforcement is haphazard and inadvertent, it is likely to produce a strange mixture of behaviors. As research shows, undesirable behaviors can be established just as readily as desirable behaviors when they are rewarded, and desirable behaviors can be extinguished as readily as undesirable behaviors when they are unrewarded. In a school with a high proportion of reluctant learners, this can create chaos.

We know, for instance, that many of the disruptive behaviors exhibited by students are the result of inadvertent reward by teachers. The teacher's attention to the behavior, no matter how unpleasant it is intended to be, often serves to reinforce the student by enhancing his daring image in the eyes of admiring peers. In the typical classroom, it is difficult for a teacher to control the types of behaviors he or she rewards, even if he or she is aware of the reinforcement process. So, when the reinforcers seem to be backfiring, and large numbers of students are unproductive, if not blatantly hostile, it is sometimes necessary to create an environment in the school which permits more careful control of what is rewarded.

Almost any veteran teacher will readily acknowledge that there must be an essential order maintained in any class if adequate academic learning is to take place. Ideally, this order should evolve from the nature of the curriculum itself and the talents of the teacher in putting it across, but conditions in a school often militate heavily against such a development. Even if we eliminated incompetent educators and archaic curricula, there would still be reluctant learners. Problems will persist as long as schools fail to provide for students who are not intrinsically reinforced by academic work—who do not experience that elusive "joy of learning." It is these students who drop out or who hang around to threaten the learning environment, as they engage in a frenzied pursuit of their own brand of reward, usually based on peer approval. If the school is unyielding in its rewards, the peer group often becomes the main source of supply and the school the object of disdain. To the dismay of parents and teachers alike, more students each year seem to be falling seriously behind in their skill development, while their social patterns become increasingly dominated by verbal and physical abuse. It is simply not enough to propose that students be "made" to learn again, or that the schools once again instill pride in learning. The fact is that the schools must be made reinforcing, one way or another, or all efforts at "reform" are likely to fail.

The schools must, therefore, seek out new arrangements of reinforcement for their alienated students. If students are not rewarded "by learning for its own sake," then they must be offered a different "pay-off" for learning. It is not enough to suggest that the lessons themselves must simply be made more reinforcing, because reluctant learners are often not willing to get involved in any lesson long enough to discover its reinforcing value. For these students, other rewards must be found. In fact, most students, if not all students at some point in their lives, depend upon some type of extrinsic reward for their school work, whether it be a good grade, praise from parent or teacher, or approval of peers.

Most students, whether they are reluctant or eager to learn, enjoy participating in a token economy system. It should be emphasized, however, that the system is not really necessary for students who are already reinforced by the school environment. The token economy is an *alternative* arrangement of reinforcers for students who do not find school rewarding. Ideally, therefore, the system should be reserved primarily for reluctant learners, while the other students continue with existing programs. It is not always possible or desirable, however, to regroup students in this manner. Consequently, teachers may wish to use a token economy with an entire group, even if only a substantial minority really need it. This may be the only realistic way to establish the type of orderly, productive, and creative environment which will benefit all the students in the long run. The eager students will simply be receiving a bonus while the reluctant students will be getting essential reinforcement for constructive involvement in class activity.

To some critics, this whole notion of "paying off" smacks of bribery. Such a criticism ignores, of course, the obvious fact that the schools and the work world have long relied upon extrinsic reward (from gold stars to money) to promote achievement and success. If all the "pay-offs" for desirable behavior were to be removed from the school, on the grounds that they constituted bribery, it would be a sterile and unproductive place indeed. It is also somewhat curious to find that many of the critics who readily extol the virtues of the free enterprise system, rich in its work incentives, are offended when some of the same principles are applied to the school setting. Besides, the use of the term "bribery" is really misplaced to begin with. Bribery refers to paying someone to engage in undesirable or illegal behavior, which is quite contrary to what the token economy attempts to do.

The only real alternative to providing more meaningful rewards is the imposition of ever more severe punitive measures, and the systematic "weeding out" of the school population. Despite the many adherents to such an approach, present legal strictures and community pressures make it an implausible, if not inhumane, plan of attack. Another obvious problem with the approach is that many learning problems are not amenable to punishment. A student suffering from a learning disability cannot simply be "forced" to do better. He can, however, be reinforced to gradually learn more. This raises the whole question of what to do with handicapped students. It is fast becoming a major problem for schools, as the movement for "mainstreaming" gains momentum and legal force. Unless preparations are made to provide for more reinforcing environments, many of these students too will join the ranks of the alienated and will become either disruptive or irrelevant to the general life of the school.

Sometimes all that is necessary is the addition of more social-type extrinsic rewards (verbal and non-verbal teacher "pay-offs"), or the updating of the traditional, albeit extrinsic, practices of evaluating and providing recognition. In some situations, however, where the students are unaccustomed or unresponsive to social rewards, the reinforcers may have to be more tangible. This is where the token economy comes into play. It provides an orderly and exciting method for offering "pay-offs" for productive student behavior. Actually, the notion of using tokens is not even novel—gold stars and letter grades have long served as tokens of achievement. The total economic framework of the system does, however, seem to add a compelling feature to this old idea.

The goal of a token economy system is not just to teach students to enjoy pay-offs for their work product, it is to enable them to see that they can indeed succeed at school work, that they can develop competencies which have even greater reward potential, and that they can actually feel good about school. In other words, the token economy is designed to provide rewards for basic behaviors which, over time, may become self-rewarding. This goal will not be achieved with every student, but at least every student will have a good chance at success.

II.

OPERATIONAL DESCRIPTION

A token economy system is an orderly arrangement of the school environment to provide reinforcement for specified academic and social behaviors. Based on the learning principles which have emerged from the work of B. F. Skinner and others, the token economy is a means for supplying positive consequences for productive behavior and for withholding reward from unproductive behavior. In other words, the system provides a network of "pay-offs" for desirable behavior, while avoiding the inadvertent reinforcement of undesirable behaviors. The system also permits more immediate reward than is possible in the typical classroom environment. It establishes clear expectations for student behavior and insures that the expression of these behaviors is reinforcing.

As with the American economy, the system described here relies on the use of tokens as tangible symbols of the things an individual wishes to possess. Using points or chips, instead of money, the tokens serve as the medium of exchange for back-up material items and special activities. The tokens also serve as the basis for evaluating student academic performance and for the distribution of various awards for achievement.

By using tokens, the student can be reinforced repeatedly and systematically every day for exhibiting a whole range of specified behaviors. Tokens make the process of reinforce-

11

ment manageable for teachers and meaningful for students. The system has relevance because it parallels the economic arrangements of our society. Through the use of a banking procedure, in which students are taught to keep track of their accumulated earnings, savings, and expenditures, the students are exposed, in a rudimentary way, to the handling of their own financial affairs. The system as a whole utilizes many of the same types of economic incentives which form the basis of the adult world of work.

Briefly stated, the token economy system operates in the following manner: As the student engages in the specified behaviors (such as arriving on time, concentrating on tasks, listening to instructions), the teacher circulates about the area giving tokens (points are used in most systems) as the behaviors are performed. The students also receive equivalent points for the work they turn in. All the points received are transferred by the students to their bank records under points earned and added into a savings balance. The teachers keep a separate record of earned points for grading purposes, leaving the students free to spend their points in any manner they choose, without affecting their grades. To spend points, the students fill out a coupon, deduct the amount on the bank record, and bring the coupon to the chosen activity (lounge, store, or outdoor events). The students with the highest accumulated earned points receive bimonthly positive letters to be taken home, with accompanying bonus points, as well as the highest letter grades at the end of each marking period.

According to basic reinforcement principles, the points are distributed when the desired behaviors occur, and are withheld when they do not. Thus, a teacher will skip by a student who is failing to perform the specified behavior, and will return with a point only when the behavior is performed. As a rule, the teachers will also attempt to ignore minor inappropriate behaviors, on the theory that teacher attention to them would simply be rewarding. So, where possible, students are not rewarded and may even be ignored, when they fail to perform desired behaviors. For behaviors which are too persistent, too disruptive, or potentially too harmful to be avoided, the students are sent immediately to an area called "time out." This is a screened area located away from all class activity, where the student must sit to await return to class. The teacher permits return when the student has ceased the undesirable behavior, or has made a commitment to do so upon his or her return. The principle operating here is to withdraw the student from the rewarding consequences of his or her behavior until the behavior is once again appropriate.

For descriptive purposes, the token economy system itself can be divided into five major components:

1. Rewards
2. Target Behaviors
3. Token Delivery Procedures
4. Token Exchange Procedures
5. Evaluation Methods

Rewards

As has already been pointed out, the tokens used in the system, whether they are points, chips, signatures, or any other symbol, are in themselves rewards. They come to have reinforcing value because, like money, they represent the things that can be purchased with them. Thus, the accumulation of tokens becomes an inherently valuable activity for the students.

The program which serves as the model for this system has utilized both points and poker chips as tokens, and some comment should be made about the relative utility of each type.

Both chips and points are effective in contained classroom settings. In open-space arrangements, with larger groups of students, however, points are the preferred token. In most classroom situations, a chip system will also require an additional operator (teacher or aide) to help administer it. As a general rule, a chip system cannot be operated effectively by a single teacher if the group exceeds 15 students. Beyond that number, the teacher simply has too much to handle to distribute chips as well as carry on instruction.

Since plastic chips are a more concrete symbol of reward than points, they tend to be most enjoyed by students from early elementary grades through the sixth grade. Chips are workable for seventh and eighth graders, but they are more likely to find the chips too "babyish." Retarded students may, however, enjoy the chips until a much older age.

Points will work quite well with younger students, so they can be readily adopted if your group is too large for a chip system. Points should be the token of choice for older students, not only for the reason already stated, but because points tend to parallel more closely the type of evaluation systems (grading and rating) in the typical school or work environment to which the student will be going eventually.

There are a variety of other types of tokens which might be created, and many could probably be plugged into the system described here. Some of these might be as traditional as gold stars, or might be as "real life" as actual money; other possibilities might include stamps, play money, marbles, cards, checkers, teacher initials or signatures, or beads.

The selection of back-up rewards is, of course, a crucial ingredient for the entire system. A system that depends on only a few scattered rewards, with a long wait before they are available, is likely to die a quick and painful death. Most students who are selected for a token program are likely to need immediate reinforcement (a reason for using tokens in the first place) and will need to have ready access to desirable back-up reinforcers within short periods of time. A good system has rewards which are available and easily earned on a daily basis, with other more valuable items and activities available on a more deferred basis.

The types of rewards utilized in a system, aside from the tokens themselves, fall into these categories:

1. teacher praise and attention
2. material items
3. activities
4. special privileges
5. awards
6. grades
7. edibles

Each of these categories is detailed in the Design Format section, so for now only a few comments are necessary. The most important consideration in selecting rewards is that they be perceived by the students to be enjoyable, valuable, and accessible. In order to "find something for everyone," the rewards must come in various forms, with new items added at timely moments throughout the year.

The purchase of the reward items to be included in the program obviously takes money, which must be obtained from a school or community source. This is the only significant cost in the entire program, however, so from an economic standpoint it is a real bargain, especially when measured against the cost of other types of alternative programs. But, bargain or not, you will still have to come up with approximately $6.00 per student per year to operate the complete program described here.

Target Behaviors

These are the student behaviors which are specified by the teachers as subject to token reinforcement. The behaviors are selected because they are regarded as essential for successful performance in the school or work environment. Since many students do not have these behaviors even weakly established in their repertoire, the tokens often must be presented for the successive approximation of the full target responses. In other words, the students are rewarded as they get closer to the expected behavior. The categories of behavior usually isolated for targeting are:

1. attendance and punctuality
2. preparedness
3. responsiveness
4. cooperativeness
5. involvement in work
6. quality and quantity of performance

Given these or other categories of target behavior, the teachers then refine the student responses which are expected, and specify the conditions under which the tokens are to be provided. To help with this refinement process, the teachers, counselors, or administrators might use a technique known as baselining. This is an observation procedure which provides specific information on the frequency and duration of problem behaviors and the environmental factors which seem to be shaping and maintaining them. Essentially, it involves the systematic recording of occurrences of inappropriate school responses over a period of time. The procedures are detailed in Figure 1.

After determining the specific target behaviors, a list is compiled for the students denoting the relative token value of each behavior. This list, which is purposely kept short and precise, also serves as the basic set of student rules for the program. The students are thereby informed in advance of exactly what is expected of them and how much the proper performance of the behaviors is worth in tokens.

Figure 1

Baseline Procedure

There are two main ways to gather data on the frequency and/or duration of problem behaviors in the school: you can observe specific individuals and record the occurrences of designated problem behaviors, or you can observe an entire group and, without regard to who exhibits particular responses, record the overall occurrences of certain problem behaviors. For this program, you might wish to gather both types of data. The individual data will, however, be the most important for measuring outcomes and for justifying your results in experimental terms. Since it may not be possible to baseline the responses of all the students who are potential candidates for your program, you should at least attempt to select a representative sample. You may have to baseline the individuals you miss at a later time, after you have actually made your selection of students, and if you need further data to prepare individual objectives. The group data will have little experimental significance unless your groups are already homogeneous and are operating under the same set of circumstances which will prevail in your program, except for the token system itself, of course. But even though you are not likely to have such control over your variables, the group data (even if only a portion of the observed group is likely to end up in your program) can give you some useful information. These gross figures may give you a good idea about which problem behaviors are most pervasive and need the most changing, and it will also give you an informal basis for judging the initial effectiveness of your token intervention. To gather this data, you might first observe the class and make notes about the problem behaviors which seem to disrupt the learning process the most; then you can select the major behaviors to follow and obtain specific baseline information.

General Baseline Procedure

1. Select the problem behaviors to be recorded (single observable acts).

2. Determine the observation schedule (the intervals of time for which you will be recording the responses).

3. Design an appropriate baseline chart and graph on which to report the occurrences of the problem behaviors.

(Continued on next page)

Figure 1 (Continued)

4. Attempt to make the observations in the least conspicuous manner (to avoid unnatural acting out).

5. Make regular notations about the events which seem to cue the occurrence of problem behaviors (the environmental conditions or consequences which appear to stimulate the behaviors). Try to determine what has happened immediately before and after the occurrence of the behavior which might have cued the response.

It is often easiest to use a chart to actually record the behaviors as they occur and then later transfer the data to a graph for each student or a whole group.

For gathering frequency data, you might use a simple chart like:

1st Interval	2nd Interval	3rd Interval	
20 minutes	20 minutes	20 minutes	
ЖНТ ЖНТ ΙΙ	ЖНТ ЖНТ	ЖНТ ЖНТ ΙΙΙΙ	

Each time the student exhibits the behavior during the interval of observation, you make a mark in the interval box (or you can keep track on a mechanical counter and simply report the total number in the box). At the end of each session, you count the marks in each box and transfer the information to a graph, such as:

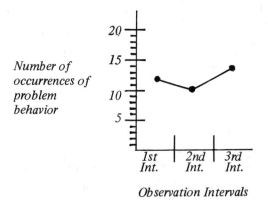

Number of occurrences of problem behavior

Observation Intervals

(Continued on next page)

Figure 1 (Continued)

For gathering duration data on problem behaviors, you can use basically the same method as above:

1st Interval   2nd Interval   3rd Interval

20 min.					20 min.						20 min.						
40	20	30	10		100	50	40	20	60	10	180	25	40	50	30	25	170	

Total   Total   Total

Each time the behavior occurs within the observation interval, you time its duration (wristwatch or stopwatch) and write the time in a portion of the interval box. You then total the seconds or minutes within each box and transfer it to a graph:

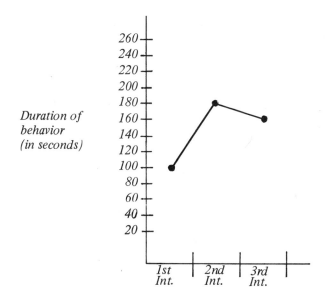

Observation Intervals

(Continued on next page)

Figure 1 (Continued)

When you take baseline data after the token system has been imple-
mented, you should use the same procedures to record the same problem behaviors. This should give you a good graphic illustration of the
reduction of problem behaviors, if all has gone well. A comparison of
data taken before and after implementation may look something like
this:

Before   *After*

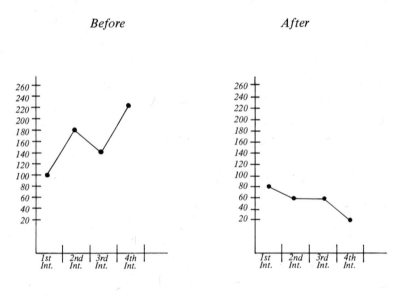

Token Delivery Procedures

After determining the type of token to be used in the system, and the complexity of the behaviors to be targeted, the actual mechanics of the token delivery system are devised. This entails the development of various charts, forms, or paraphernalia for distributing the tokens to each student, depending on the nature of the system. Illustrations and directions for this phase of planning are available in the Design Format section.

The schedules for distributing the tokens are a matter for careful consideration. In the initial stages of a token economy, it is usually best to reward most target behaviors immediately after they occur (or as closely as possible), except for behaviors which are expected to occur for extended periods of time (such as on-task responses). Behaviors which have a long duration are usually rewarded on an interval basis, while behaviors which have only brief and infrequent expression are rewarded on a ratio basis (each expression of the behavior equals a certain number of tokens). After a program progresses, is it often possible, and even desirable, to change the schedules of reinforcement by altering the ratios (increasing the number of responses per token) and lengthening the intervals (increasing the length of time between tokens).

Some token economy systems can actually be phased out of existence over time, as the need for token reinforcement decreases and other extrinsic, but more social, rewards take over importance, coupled with intrinsic reinforcement which the students themselves may now be supplying. This can be a realistic goal for many programs, but it all depends, of course, on the capacities of the students involved. However, even if the elimination of the program does not seem feasible, it is still important to make the class environment as representative as possible of the outside world, while retaining its reinforcing quality, so the students' eventual entry into other environments will not be shocking.

The gradual elimination of the number of tokens provided (called fading) can usually best be accomplished with groups of students who are relatively homogeneous and who are working on only a few major behavior patterns. Groups which are more heterogeneous and are working on a broader range of problem behaviors are likely to present more difficulties for fading. Usually, the most realistic alternative in this situation is to phase the students themselves into other programs as they develop the necessary exit behaviors, and then maintain the system for those who are not ready to leave.

Token Exchange Procedures

As with the delivery procedure, the exchange procedure requires the creation of various charts and forms, which are also detailed in the Design Format. For now, suffice it to say that the exchange of tokens revolves around the use of a bank record. On the record, the student keeps track of his or her earnings and transactions on a daily basis. Each week the teachers verify the student's records and transfer the accumulated balances to new record sheets. Thus, the student is able to clearly see how his earnings balance increases through the year and how his savings balance is affected by his expenditures. The bank record also indicates how well the student is doing in the competition for positive letters, trophies, and other special awards.

The students carry their point sheet and bank record to each class. After the tokens have been distributed in the classes, the student totals his or her earnings and transfers them to the appropriate boxes on the bank record. A coupon system is used in conjunction with the bank record for making purchases at the store and for gaining entry into the lounge and other special activities. Time is provided at the beginning and end of each day for reconciling balances and for making purchases. The records are then left in the class area when the students leave for the day.

Evaluation Methods

The structure for your token economy system will be influenced by the evaluation methods you choose or are compelled to use by the school system. The methods you choose should account for three main aspects of your program:

1. measuring students academic and social behavior
2. reporting student performance to parents and others
3. measuring the overall effectiveness of the program itself

Since the specifics of the various evaluation methods are discussed in the Design Format section, only a few general remarks are needed here. For measuring individual student behavior change, you can make comparisons of baseline data, administrative records, and teacher anecdotal records, as well as using norm- and criterion-referenced tests. For reporting student performance, you can use a variety of techniques (most of them really quite traditional, but with new wrinkles): letter grades, teacher comments, parent conferences, home visits, behavior checklists, and letters to parents. To measure the overall effectiveness of the program itself, you will probably want to rely upon many of the same methods you have used for measuring individual progress, but with reference to total group scores. You might wish to add an attitude survey of the group's feelings about themselves and their progress.

Regardless of the combination of methods employed, it should be remembered that a token economy sets out to make deliberate changes in a variety of specific behaviors, so accurate and thorough data is essential. For other educational approaches, this not such a critical need, because they are often based upon such high-sounding goals that they are, by their nature, unmeasurable. Unfortunately, with these programs no one knows, after all is said and done, whether any change has really occurred in the students. This raises serious questions of accountability and generalizability.

III.

DESIGN FORMAT

Now that you have an overview of the token economy, you are ready to flesh out the finer details of the system. As has been pointed out, the system described in this book is based on work done in an open-space middle school (sixth, seventh, and eighth grades) over the last several years. Each year approximately 100 students have been involved in the program at one time. Since the program's inception, the whole system as well as various components have been adopted in a number of other schools. The details follow.

Rewards

You should compile an exhaustive list of potential rewards for your students and then purchase a small supply of what you anticipate will be most appealing, so that you can show the students on the first day that you are ready to start and are not just making promises. You should discuss the types of rewards you would like to make available and then solicit student requests. This student input is important to make them feel part of the system from the beginning. It will be helpful to tell the students your total budget and your money limits for individual material items and special activities. Permit the students to propose a list and then vote on the top-priority items. You might do this repeatedly during the year to keep the incentives strong and the students involved.

For the model program, the following rewards have been employed:
   A. Letter Grades
   B. Store Items
   C. Auctions
   D. Lounge
   E. Super Letters
   F. Trophies and Certificates
   G. Miscellaneous Events

A. *Letter Grades*

Letter grades are used only on report cards at the end of each marking period. The students receive points on their work during the marking period which are later translated into letter grades. The general criteria for points on assignments are:

   0 points — Assignment is not 1/2 complete and nearly all incorrect.
   1 point — assignment is about 1/2 complete with only some of it correct.
   2 points — assignment is nearly complete and about 1/2 correct.
   3 points — assignment is complete and over 1/2 correct.
   4 points — assignment is complete and correct.

The points are entered by the students into their bank records as earnings and may be spent on desired items. This way the students perceive grading as basically a rewarding affair, without the usual aversive implications and hostile reactions. The points accumulated in each subject area during a marking period are then tallied to determine the letter grades. The highest point earners receive "A's," next highest "B's," and so on. This method permits students to stay competitive, even when their abilities vary widely.

The critical feature here is the nature of the curriculum

chosen for the program. It is important that the students see their initial learning tasks as readily surmountable. This is necessary because the students you are likely to be working with will tend to be easily frustrated and defeated. They must think that they can master the task in a short period of time and be almost guaranteed positive feedback, in the form of teacher praise and tokens. As time passes, the lessons should be made more complex and the evaluation criteria raised.

B. *Store Items*

A store can be easily set up in a metal cabinet (which locks), or a structure can be built by the students themselves, if they have the ability. The store should contain a variety of material items at a range of prices. It is a good idea to stock the store with essential school supplies (pencils, pens, crayons, erasers, notebooks, etc.) as well as other perhaps more popular items. With basic supplies available in the store, priced very reasonably (in tokens, of course), you can then require students to be prepared completely for class each day. To insure this, you should give your students a short period of time (3-5 minutes), before instruction begins for the day, to purchase necessary items. If a student then begins class without required materials, you should sell the item at double the token price and skip the first point of the day.

It is easiest to operate a store if you are able to use student volunteers or qualifiers as storekeepers. The store should be open during non-instructional periods, usually immediately before and after the day's classes, a time you might call "homebase." To purchase an item from the store, the student must present to the storekeeper a teacher-verified coupon with the appropriate amount properly designated. A price list should be prominently displayed and circulated to all students, so that they can decide what they want and its cost before they go to the store area. The storekeeper should initial the in-coming coupons to cancel them and then retain them for cross-checking transactions, if necessary.

Below is a composite price list of store items which have been employed in the model program.

	Items	*Points*
1.	White Notebook Paper (each sheet)	1
2.	Color Notebook Paper (each sheet)	2
3.	Pencil	15
4.	Pencil Tip Eraser	20
5.	Large Eraser	35
6.	Barrettes	40
7.	Mechanical Pencil Lead	50
8.	Small Notepad	60
9.	Fuzzy Patches	60
10.	Wood Ruler	70
11.	Ink Pen	75
12.	Insect Pencil Sharpener	90
13.	Felt Pen	100
14.	School Folder	100
15.	Notebook Zipper Pockets	125
16.	Math Compass	125
17.	Small Hairbrush	125
18.	Football Kicking Tee	125
19.	Mini Playing Cards	150
20.	Mechanical Pencil	200
21.	Regular Playing Cards	250
22.	Stationary	275
23.	"For Sale" Signs	300
24.	Pierced Earrings	300
25.	Sew-On Patches	300
26.	Head Sweat Bands	300
27.	Wrist Sweat Bands	450
28.	Miniature Magnetic Games (Chess and Checkers)	500
29.	Stapler and Staples	500
30.	45 rpm Record	500
31.	Model	600
32.	Pad Lock	800
33.	Bike Lock	1,000
34.	Baseball	1,000

During the year you can expect to spend at least 40% of your total budget on store items.

The easiest method for pricing your rewards is to work out a simple ratio of how many points will compare with the actual money value of the item (5 points per 1¢). It is not always possible, or necessarily desirable to stick to the ratio, however. You may wish to be flexible, because on certain occasions you might want to make expensive items more accessible in order to build interest. Also, the cheapest items should generally be essential school supplies. For pricing all the items, it is often best to price the cheapest and most expensive items first and work toward the moderate items. The price of special activities should also bear some relationship to the price of store items, so the economy seems a coherent whole to the students.

C. Auctions

Every few weeks you should consider holding an auction for all the students in the program. In the model program, one of the teachers serves as an auctioneer and sells five or six items to the highest bidders. The items vary in value, from cheap "white elephants" to expensive fads, and are different from the items available in the store. At each auction at least one of the items is of particular value to the students, usually because they have asked for it, and its availability has been announced long before the auction, to obtain maximum incentive from it.

To bid at the auction, the students come together in a large group meeting with their bank records in hand. The auctioneer holds up each item with an opening amount and then the students stand up and yell their bids. The students are free to bid to the limits of their savings balances. The bidding works best if no more than 50 points may be offered over the previous bid. This prevents a student from automatically escalating the bidding to an uncontested level and taking all the fun out of the process. As the students win an item, the amount is immediately deducted from their savings balance on the bank record, as they come to claim it.

This will no doubt prove to be a very popular activity, and your most costly single event. If you hold an auction every three to four weeks, you should plan to spend at least 1/3 your total budget. In the model program, involving 100 students, the total budget was $600.00 and the auction allowance was $200.00 (between $10.00 and $20.00 per auction). This total amount will vary, of course, with the size of your student population. For smaller programs, the proportion of the budget will have to be somewhat larger, since you will need at least $8.00 for a good auction, regardless of the size of the group (unless you use donated or used items). On the final day of school, a clearance auction should be held so that the students can spend all remaining tokens. For this event, you might sell leftover items from the store, games from the lounge, and donated items. The students should be informed in advance that this event will take place at the end of the year.

Below is a list of items which proved most desirable for auction in the model program:
1. Skateboard
2. Transistor Radio
3. Posters
4. Camera
5. Calculator
6. Record Album
7. Microscope
8. Baseball Bat
9. Books (puzzles, comics, fiction)
10. Ugly Rubber Creatures
11. Felt Pen Sets

12. 10-Pocket Folders
13. Hats
14. Globe
15. Autographs of Celebrities
16. Football
17. Jewelry
18. Sea Monkies
19. Puzzles
20. T-Shirts
21. Board Games
22. Pennants
23. Sun Glasses
24. Large Models
25. Yo-Yo
26. Craft Kits
27. Gift Certificates
28. Sports Tickets
29. Fishing Tackle
30. Stamp and Coin Collections

D. *Lounge*

In the model program, a student lounge has been partitioned off in an area away from the classes. For a price of 125 points, the students are allowed to opt out of a class to enter the lounge. During the initial homebase, the students must secure a coupon for 125 points, which is then presented to the teacher at the beginning of the chosen class.

The following activities are permitted in the lounge:

1. watching television
2. playing board games
3. eating food
4. drawing on a chalkboard
5. reading magazines

6. listening to records
7. just talking

E. *"Super Letters"*

In the model program, an honors meeting is held every two weeks to distribute "Super Letters" and to announce the candidates for trophies. Each student who has earned the pre-announced number of qualification points (total number earned over a two-week period), and who has not been in "time out" more than once during that period, receives a "Super Letter." The 15 highest point earners (out of 100 students) are given "Top 15" letters, and all remaining qualifiers receive regular letters. In the bonus box on the letter, the five highest earners receive a 50 point bonus, the next five receive 40 points, the next five receive 30 points, and all the rest receive 20 point bonuses. The bonuses are transferred by the students to their bank record bonus box and then added into the savings balance. The bonuses are not counted as earnings, since this would tend to distort the evaluation system and perpetuate the same students in the top spots.

Both types of letters are illustrated in Figure 2.

F. *Trophies and Certificates*

At each honors meeting, after all the letters have been publically announced, the "Top 15" for the semester is then read off and distributed to all the students. To qualify for the list, the students' total earnings for the semester to date must land them among the top 15 point earners in all classes combined. As these points accumulate, the relative positions of the students fluctuate during the semester. The students who finally end up in the top three positions at the end of the semester receive trophies with the inscription "Super Student." The remaining 12 students receive certificates of achievement at a special honors meeting. The principal often

Figure 2

"Super Letters"

"Top 15" Letter

. . . .
Evaluation Period

Dear Parents:

We are extremely happy to inform you that your student, ...
. . . . , has done an excellent job in pod classes
this evaluation period. Your student has worked hard in math, language
arts, reading, social studies and skills. We are particularly pleased that
your student has cooperated so well with teachers and fellow students.

We know that you are as happy as we are with this successful performance. You can expect one of these letters every two weeks, if your
student has properly earned it.

Thank you for your encouragement at home.

```
* * * * * * *          Sincerely,
*         *            The Pod Teachers
* Bonus *
*         *
* * * * * * *
```

Super Letter

. . . .
Evaluation Period

Dear Parents:

We are happy to inform you that your student, ...
. . . ., has done a satisfactory job in pod classes
this evaluation period. Your student has worked hard in math, language
arts, reading, social studies and skills. We are particularly pleased that
your student has cooperated so well with teachers and fellow students.

We know you are as happy as we are with this successful performance. You can expect one of these letters every two weeks, if your
student has properly earned it.

Thank you for your encouragement at home.

```
* * * * * * *          Sincerely,
*         *            The Pod Teachers
* Bonus *
*         *
* * * * * * *
```

comes in to make the formal presentations. At the beginning of each semester, the students' earnings balances (not savings) then return to zero and the competition begins anew.

G. *Miscellaneous Events*

Following is a list of activities which have been included or proposed during the initial years of the model program.

1. *Softball.* For 300 points the students may opt out of two class periods to play softball on the school grounds. Twice a month during the spring months, the first twenty students to make a paid reservation are eligible to go out.

2. *Raffle (proposal).* Numbered tickets might be sold through the store or through some other distribution method. The students purchase tickets for a fixed price (tokens, of course) and place 1/2 the numbered ticket into a big bin or jar. Every two or four weeks a drawing is to be held and prizes awarded to the winners. Caution should be exercised with this particular activity, however. It should not be used in communities which might be resistant to any form of gambling.

3. *Field Trips.* The first three students to earn a pre-announced number of points during a four week period are eligible to purchase (150 points) a trip to lunch at a fast food restaurant with one of the teachers. This activity does, however, raise questions of legal liability for student travel in a teacher's car, if one is used. This type of qualification procedure can be used for a whole range of other field trips for small or large groups of students. Events worth considering are: movies, picnics, sports contests, and bowling.

4. *Break Periods.* In classrooms where a lounge is not practicable, a break period can be established. The students as a group might be permitted to earn minutes for the break period each day. Group contingencies can be arranged whereby a minute of break is earned each time students as

a whole perform specified tasks. The minutes might be accumulated on the chalkboard or on a model clock. If breaks can be taken outside the room, and if more than one adult is involved in the program, individual contingencies can be employed—which are really preferable to group contingencies. At the beginning of each day a point target can be announced and each student who has reached it by the specified time is permitted to take the break, while the others remain behind to work. Break activities might include:

1. chalkboard writing
2. board games
3. card playing
4. puzzles
5. records and dancing
6. filmstrips
7. outdoor sports

Group contingencies can also be employed for special activities. The students might be divided into small groups of three to five members, according to desk or table seating. At the end of each day, the group members total up their combined earnings. When a group reaches a combined total of 100 points, it announces its achievement and an additional minute is added to the "minute wheel" for a special class party or outdoor event. Alternatively, when a group reaches 100 it might add one qualifying point for a class trip. In other words, for every 100 small group points, the full class is brought one point closer to the criterion level established for a class trip.

5. *Special Jobs.* Certain jobs are designated as rewards. Students who obtain the criterion points within a specified time limit can qualify for one of the available positions. Extra bonuses might be offered for good service in the positions. Special jobs might include: bankers, storekeepers, media operators, roll runners, or board cleaners.

6. *Special Bonuses.* For every day that no student is sent to "time out," the entire group of students receives a bonus of 25 points. This offer must, of course, be pre-announced if it is to have any influence on behavior.

The use of group contingencies, in which the whole class earns a reward if every member of the class performs the desired behavior, should be used only sparingly, and, in some circumstances, not at all. The group contingencies suggested above are only intended for use in a system which is primarily based on individual contingencies. When rewards are made contingent upon the performance of a whole group, especially if these rewards are the only ones available, there almost inevitably occurs internal struggle between students to get the dissidents "into line." Although this approach is often advocated as a good method for teaching the students to discipline themselves, it has some serious pitfalls. First, it is not really teaching self-discipline, but rather teacher-imposed group pressure—to say otherwise is intellectually dishonest. Second, this type of approach often plays into the hands of students who love to "show off." It provides a fertile opportunity for recalcitrant students to seize a great deal of inappropriate attention for holding the group hostage to their antics. In other words, the students may be more rewarded by holding the group up than by obtaining the group reward. Third, group pressure often leads to a fairly constant undertone of students telling each other to "shut up" and "get to work," which tends to take away from the type of peaceful and orderly environment aimed for under a token system.

Of all the rewards to be used in the system, the type which may ultimately prove most successful with many of the students has not even been mentioned in this discussion: social reward. The use of positive social reinforcement must not be overlooked when designing a system like this. The appropriate and systematic use of various verbal and non-verbal teacher behaviors as rewards, when paired with tokens, can be extremely effective. The critical fact here is that under a token system the teacher can more carefully focus his or her social reinforcers on developing patterns than is possible in a typical class setting. Under the system, it becomes the teacher's job to systematically reinforce a set of target behaviors and to make certain that social reinforcers are provided for each student. In the typical classroom, social reinforcement is usually haphazard and unwittingly reserved for the "elite" of the class.

One way to insure that teachers are using social reinforcers more appropriately and more often is to ask that they be used, in the beginning at least, nearly every time a token is dispensed. For instance, as the teacher gives a point for on-task behavior, he or she might say, "I really like the way you're working on this." Or, perhaps less judgmentally, the teacher might just describe what is happening, "You appear to be working really hard on this assignment." Your students should learn to make the association between the token and social reinforcers, so that they will be able to respond more readily to the social reinforcers when the non-social rewards are faded out or are unavailable in another environment.

To help clarify what social reinforcers are, the following list might be helpful:

Verbal Reinforcers
praise (spoken or written)
enjoyable conversation
special greetings
pleasant tone of voice
flattering remarks
written comments on paper
special correspondence to student or parent

Non-Verbal Reinforcers
holding eye contact
handshakes and handslaps
hugging
close physical proximity
special signals of greeting
pleasant facial expressions

Before leaving the discussion of rewards, a few closing comments should be made on the use of edibles. As a general rule, candy and soda should not be used in school token programs, even though they might be highly desired items. Recent medical studies indicate that, besides the well known dental problems caused by the sugar content, artificial coloring and flavoring agents may contribute to "hyperactivity," which may be the very behavioral reason some of the students are in your class in the first place. There are, of course, numerous types of food which might be appropriate for some programs (juices, milk, ice cream, baked goods, sugarless gum, fruit, etc.), but the model program has not used any. It was felt that food was unnecessary and would cause too many logistical problems.

Target Behaviors

Before attempting to set up a token economy system in your school, you should make some careful observations of what is actually happening in the present environment. This will help you decide if the token approach is really appropriate to deal with your particular problems. As a rule of thumb, approaches which can effectively change problem behaviors by means which do not rely upon tangible rewards should be given priority consideration. The goal of promoting a less materialistic society will obviously be better served through the use of social and academic incentives over token rewards, provided they are all that is necessary to shape the behaviors considered to be essential (which is not always the case).

If a change of behavior in a very small number of students in a given situation would permit effective learning for the rest of the group, then an individualized reinforcement program, perhaps still based on tokens, should be considered over the approach described in this book. Any such arrangement must be conducted discreetly, however, to avoid stigmatizing the participants or, more likely, creating a ripple effect, with other students clamoring to be part of the system. Individual token programs also have a way of dying out before they can accomplish much. Teachers often lose interest or find it too difficult to keep up with the system unless it is carefully coordinated.

If a basic change in the curriculum is likely to eliminate the chronic problems, then, of course, all effort should be invested in this aspect of your program and not in a token economy. This is generally the reform procedure recommended by most education commentators, and it certainly has merit for a large number of struggling students; but sometimes it is just not enough.

If you still see a compelling need for a token economy in your school, to change problem behavior and promote your educational goals, you should move to the next step of gathering baseline data. This phase will provide you with specific information on the frequency and duration of the common problem behaviors and the environmental factors which seem to stimulate and maintain them. Using a form like that provided in Figure 1, you will be able to gather objective data about what it is you will seek to change, which, in turn, will provide a means to measure at a later date whether in fact the changes have actually occurred. After you have established the token economy, you should then take baselines at various intervals on the same behaviors included in your first baseline, to determine levels of change. In an era of increased pressure for educational accountability, this matter of proving results may be absolutely essential.

Gathering data need not consume a great deal of time, perhaps a couple of weeks, depending on the size of your population. If, however, you intend to set up an experimental design, the complexity of the task may increase considerably. The degree of sophistication of your data gathering will depend entirely on your need to substantiate outcomes. At the minimum, however, your data should be complete enough to give you a clear idea about your goals for change and accurate enough to allow for follow-up comparisons.

The main virtue in gathering data in this fashion when determining the scope of your problems is that it ensures that you have information which is by its nature relatively objective. Baselining allows little room for drawing inferences about the "inner states" of the students and teachers. Your task is to graph the occurrences of observable actions, not to speculate about the "attitudes" or "feelings" of the students.

After you have decided on the general behaviors you wish to target, you should then attempt to reduce them to very specific terms and assign them appropriate token weights. A typical target behavior list presented to the students might look like this:

Class Behaviors

To earn points in this class, you must perform the following behaviors:

Be Prepared

1. Arrive in class on time (no later than 8:42 a.m.)

First   2. Sit in assigned table or desk immediately.

Point   3. Have all necessary materials (paper, pencil, books, etc.) ready before class begins.

Concentrate on Tasks

1. Listen to all instructions carefully.
2. Read, write, watch, listen, and talk at appropriate times.
3. Remain seated (except to sharpen pencil, go to bathroom,

Middle or obtain materials.)

Points 4. Work continuously.
5. Refrain from poking, hitting, pushing, tripping others.
6. Raise hands when questions or problems arise.

Clean Up

1. Hand in all work to teacher.

Last 2. Return materials to proper places.

Point 3. Pick up debris around seats.
4. Remain in seat until dismissed.

Token Delivery Procedures

If you choose to use points as your tokens, you will need:

1. Point Sheets
2. Bank Records
3. Coupons

Since this section deals primarily with delivery procedures, the bank records and coupons will be discussed under Token Exchange Procedures.

The easiest method for distributing points is for the teacher to circulate among the students making slash marks on their point sheets as they perform the target behaviors. Figures 3 and 5 illustrate the type of point sheet, with accompanying explanation, which has been used in the model program.

There are many other easily designed devices for collecting points. Index cards can be readily employed, if your system is less complex than the model. You might also consider some sort of clipboard arrangements for each student, or you might devise a ticket on which the teacher punches holes. A special rubber stamp might also make an interesting marking device. The point sheet, however, seems to serve most teachers' purposes best. (The text continues, following these figures, on page 51.)

Figure 3

Point Sheet

NAME _____   Week _____
                                      Homebase _____

MONDAY

Homebase			I		I

Math

| I | | I | | 2 | | 4 |

Social Studies

| I | I | I | | 3 | | 6 |

English

| I | I | I | | 4 | | 7 |

Reading

| I | I | I | | 3 | | 6 |

Science

| | I | I | | 3 | | 5 |

Total | 29

TUESDAY

Homebase | I | | I |

Math

| I | I | I | | 2 | | 5 |

Social Studies

| I | I | I | | 3 | | 6 |

English

| I | | I | | 4 | | 6 |

Reading

| | I | I | | 3 | | 5 |

Science

| I | I | I | | 2 | | 5 |

Total | 28

WEDNESDAY

Homebase | I | | I |

Math

| I | I | I | | 3 | | 6 |

Social Studies

| I | I | I | I | | 4 |

English

| I | I | I | | 3 | | 6 |

Reading

| | I | I | | 4 | | 6 |

Science

| I | I | | 4 | | 6 |

Total | 29

WEEK'S TOTAL

| 143 |

THURSDAY

Homebase | I | | I |

Math

| I | I | I | | 2 | | 5 |

Social Studies

| I | | I | | 4 | | 6 |

English

| | I | I | | 3 | | 5 |

Reading

| I | I | I | | 3 | | 6 |

Science

| I | I | I | | 3 | | 6 |

Total | 29

FRIDAY

Homebase | I | | I |

Math

| I | I | I | I | | 4 |

Social Studies

| I | I | I | | 3 | | 6 |

English

| I | I | | 4 | | 6 |

Reading

| I | I | I | | 3 | | 6 |

Science

| I | I | I | | 2 | | 5 |

Total | 28

Figure 3 (Continued)

Explanation of Point Sheet

1. At the beginning of each week, the students receive a new sheet in homebase group.

2. Homebase periods, the first and last events of the day, are used for student record-keeping with this point method. The teacher-operator makes a slash (equalling 1 point) in the homebase box, if the students arrive to the homebase area on time and sit in their assigned seats.

3. After receiving their homebase point, and after being dismissed, the students then pass to their class periods (rotating schedule with a varied subject order) and receive points from each teacher during each subject.

4. Under each subject, the teacher uses the first three boxes to record point marks for class behavior. The first box is used for preparation (student is on time, is in assigned seat, has materials ready). If a student lacks paper or pencil, he or she is not given first point and is required to purchase the item for double the normal price (in points). No student is permitted to begin class without necessary materials. The second box is used for points for attending to tasks (reading, writing, listening, talking) on a variable interval schedule. The number of points used for attending depends on the maturity of the program and needs of the student. 1-3 points are usually appropriate for one class period. The third box is used for clean-up purposes (turning in assignments, returning materials, picking up, etc.). Usually 1 point is provided for this purpose. The fourth box (the rectangle) is used to record assignment points. Under this system, the student may self-record points returned on assignments or the teacher may record them himself/herself on a daily or weekly basis.

5. At the end of each period, the students add the slashes (1 point each) in the first three boxes to the number in the assignment box, which gives them the total for that subject. The sum is recorded in the box to the immediate right.

6. After following the same procedure for each class, the students return to homebase to total up their points for the day (add down the right hand column).

7. Each subject total as well as the day's total is then recorded in the bank record (Figure 4).

8. At the end of each week, the students add together all the daily

(Continued on next page)

Figure 3 (Continued)

totals and report the week's total in the appropriate box. This totalling
is also done on the bank record in order to cross check the figure.

9. The students turn in both the weekly point sheet and bank record
at the end of the week for tallying, crosschecking, and transferring by
the teachers.

Figure 4

Bank Record for Points

NAME _____   WEEK _____

HOMEBASE _____

```
************    *************
*           *  *  TOTAL     *
*  BONUS    *  *  SAVINGS   *
*           *  *  BALANCE   *
************    *             *
               *    560      *
               *             *
```

DAYS				POINTS EARNED				POINTS SPENT	
	HOME-BASE	MATH	SOCIAL STUDIES	ENGLISH	READING	SCI.	TOTAL		
Monday	1	4	6	7	6	5	29	15	574
Tuesday	1	5	6	6	5	5	28		602
Wednesday	1	6	4	6	6	6	29		631
Thursday	1	5	6	5	6	6	29	30	630
Friday	1	4	6	6	6	5	28	45	613
Totals	5	24	28	30	29	27	143	90	

```
****************          ***************************          *************
*              *          *  Total Earnings For The  *          *  NEW      *
*  Honor Points *         *          Year            *          *  BALANCE  *
*              *          *                          *          *    613    *
*     120      *          *         2,920            *          *           *
*              *          *                          *          *************
****************          ***************************
```

Figure 4 (Continued)

Explanation of Bank Record for Points

1. At the beginning of each week, each student receives his or her new bank record. Already noted on the record (by a teacher-operator) is the student's current savings balance, total earnings for the year to date, and the honor points (earned toward achievement awards and "Super Letters" every two weeks).

2. After the day's classes, the student transfers his or her totals for each subject (including homebase) from the point sheet to the appropriate bank record columns.

3. The student then adds across the row to find the total for the day (which must match the total on the point sheet). The daily total is then added to the current savings balance and the sum is recorded in the far column. This procedure is repeated each day during the week.

4. If the student spends any points during the week, the number spent is recorded in the proper column (across from the day of the week) and subtracted from the current savings balance.

5. At the end of the week, during the final banking period, the student adds down each subject column to find the week's total in each class. The student then finds the week's total earnings by adding down the daily total column or by adding across the subject totals.

6. If the student has earned any bonus points for jobs performed, this should be recorded in the appropriate box and added to the current savings balance to yield the final savings balance. Bonuses are not included as earnings.

7. To cross-check the final savings balance, add the week's total earnings to the week's initial savings balance and subtract the total points spent for the week.

8. After students complete their tallying, the bank record is then turned in so that the figures can be checked and transferred.

9. A new bank record is then made up for each student with the new savings balance, the new total earnings figure (the figure in the year's total box plus the week's earning total), and the new honor points (the figure in the box plus the week's total earnings).

Figure 5

Single-Subject Point Record

Name _____

Date _____

	Earnings		Savings
	200		100

MONDAY

| I | II | I | Assignments | Total 4 | Spend | Balance 104 |

TUESDAY

| I | I | I | Assignments 4 | Total 7 | Spend 10 | Balance 101 |

WEDNESDAY

| I | II | I | Assignments | Total 4 | Spend | Balance 105 |

THURSDAY

| I | II | | Assignments 5 | Total 8 | Spend 50 | Balance 63 |

FRIDAY

| | II | I | Assignments | Total 3 | Spend | Balance 66 |

Bonus

226	60	66
Total Earnings	Total Spent	Final Savings Balance

Figure 5 (Continued)

Explanation of Single-Subject Point Record

This form is a combined point sheet and bank record and is the type that might be the easiest to use with a token system in a single-subject classroom.

1. Each week the student receives a new record with the accumulated earnings and savings balance noted in the top boxes.
2. The class behavior points are collected in the first three boxes under each day.
3. Points received on assignments are recorded in the appropriate box on the day they are returned.
4. The student adds up the points earned for each day and places the amount in the total box after each day.
5. The student then adds the new daily earnings to his or her savings balance, subtracting any points spent that day (which has already been noted in the spend box).
6. At the end of the week, the student adds the top earnings box to the daily totals to arrive at the new total earnings in the bottom box.
7. The student tallies the number of points spent for the week and puts the amount in the total spent box.
8. The student also brings his savings balance from Friday down to the final savings balance box.
9. Bonuses are recorded in the designated box and added into only the savings balance at the end of the week.

Figure 6

Bank Record for Chips
(Single or Multiple Subjects)

Name _____   Week _____

Folder _____

Previous Earnings	Previous Savings Balance
850	120

	MONDAY	TUESDAY	WEDNESDAY	THURSDAY	FRIDAY	TOTALS
Number of chips left over from previous day A	Last Balance 120	Last Balance 135	Last Balance 165	Last Balance 182	Last Balance 214	
Number of chips earned each day B	Chips Earned 25	Chips Earned 30	Chips Earned 27	Chips Earned 32	Chips Earned 30	Total chips earned for the week 144
Number of chips spent each day C	Chips Spent 10	Chips Spent 0	Chips Spent 10	Chips Spent 0	Chips Spent 25	Total chips spent for the week 45
Total Number of chips remaining after the day's work D	New Balance 135	New Balance 165	New Balance 182	New Balance 214	New Balance 219	Final Balance 219

To find the New Balance each day:

A + B - C = D

Bonus

Figure 6 (Continued)

Explanation of Bank Record for Chips

1. At the beginning of each week, each student receives his or her new bank record, noting the previous savings balance and total previous earnings. The student immediately follows the arrow to Monday and transfers the savings balance to the first row (A).

2. At the end of each day the student counts his or her chips and records the total earned in the proper daily row (B). The student then turns in all the chips.

3. If the student spends any chips, the number spent is recorded under the proper day in the appropriate row (C).

4. At the end of each day the student adds his or her chips earned (row B) to the last balance (row A), subtracts any chips spent (row C), and finds the new balance (row D). The student then follows the arrow and places the new balance on the top of the next day's work. The same procedure is followed for each day of the week.

5. During the final banking period of the week, the student merely moves the new savings balance to the totals column. The student then adds across the row (B) to find the total earned for the week, and adds across the row (C) to find the total spent as well. If the student has earned bonus chips for job performance, the number is recorded in the designated box.

6. After all tallying is complete, the student turns in the bank record for checking and transferring. The teacher-operator then makes a new bank record for each student with the new figures in the previous earnings box and the previous savings balance (add in bonuses).

7. This banking method does not provide a running total of earnings in each subject area, so this will have to be kept independently if the form is used for multiple subjects.

Your schedules for point reinforcement are likely to vary with the type of behaviors you are targeting. Some behaviors (like arriving on time or bringing proper materials) are best rewarded on a fixed ratio (one or more points per each occurrence of the behavior). Other behaviors (like concentrating on the learning tasks) need to be rewarded on an interval schedule. Most fixed interval schedules (for instance, one point every ten minutes) are not desirable for school token economies. The students too often pick up the rhythm of the schedule and tend to slacken their performance until just before the point is dispensed, then making a sudden burst of activity until the point is given, followed by a slackening after receiving the point. A variable interval is usually much more effective, since the students cannot predict when the points are actually coming. One time a point may be given after only a few minutes of work, while another time it might be as long as ten minutes, depending on the number being given out in the system. This interval method is also preferable because it does not lock the teachers into a pattern which is likely to interfere with instruction and class activity.

If you wish to set up a token economy utilizing poker chips, you will need a set of colored chips and carpenter nail belts for each teacher. Under this method, the teachers circulate among the students, drawing the chips from their belts, and handing the chips to the students as they perform the target behaviors. The students collect the chips during the course of the day (in containers, if necessary) and then turn them in after recording their earnings on the bank record (in Figure 6).

A typical chip system might assign values to the chips as follows:

white chip = 1
blue chip = 5
red chip = 10

This is done in order to reduce the total number of chips students must accumulate during the day, and it also simulates more closely a money system. The teachers move about the room exchanging the higher valued chips for their equivalent in lower denominations. To operate a chip system for 25 students, you will need at least 100 white chips, 75 blue chips, and 60 red chips. The supply you need will vary, of course, with your reward procedures.

Regardless of the type of token you employ, you should make it clear to the students from the outset that the values for the target behaviors and the price of the rewards may change as the year progresses. This way you will be free to fade tokens, if it is feasible, and you will not be locked into rewarding only a static set of target behaviors, as well as being able to manipulate prices according to your budgetary restraints. You should always start out by rewarding most generously the behaviors you consider most critical. As time passes, the behaviors you consider critical are likely to change and become more complex. This should be taken as a sign of success.

You should also inform the class that each student sometimes has different behaviors he needs to work on the most, so no one should be surprised if classmates receive tokens at different times. You should, however, avoid this for those social behaviors required to maintain basic order. What you do not want to happen is for one student to notice that another is getting more tokens than him for, say, showing up on time or staying in his seat. His reaction might be to turn up late or jump out of his seat repeatedly in hopes of getting on the other schedule.

As much as possible, however, you will want to keep your delivery schedules flexible. You should specify a set of target behaviors with assigned values, like that provided in the Target Behavior section, but this should not necessarily prohibit you from giving tokens for more subtle responses and at less predetermined times.

Even if you do not intend to use tokens as your basis for grading, you should still give them for work output. This actually parallels more closely what happens in work environments than does providing tokens for performing social behaviors. The most important consideration is that you attempt to pay out for assignments on the spot. Assignments should be returned promptly with the designated number of points on the paper, or with the amount of chips physically dispensed upon return or completion of the assignment. For oral work, the tokens may also be distributed as the behaviors (discussing, listening, watching) are occurring. The tokens should also be used to make previously unpalatable tasks more enjoyable. For instance, a large bonus might be offered for demonstrating competency with the multiplication facts, or for passing a spelling or functional reading test.

It is not enough, however, just to know when to dispense tokens. Anyone who operates a token economy system should also have a basic understanding of reinforcement principles. Since the professed goal of the system is to change behavior, you should know why it happens. You should be able to make deliberate choices about how the processes are used, instead of relying on just the system itself to control student behavior. Since only a brief discussion can be provided here, you should consult the reference section for books which give a thorough background.

Reinforcement Processes

It is easiest to think of reinforcement processes in terms of strengthening and weakening behaviors. If you wish to use reinforcement to strengthen a response, or its nearest approximation, the behavior should be followed as soon as possible by a pleasant event (consequence). This is where you intervene with the tokens, the back-up rewards, and your social reinforcers. To weaken an undesirable response, you will use either negative reinforcement, non-reinforcement, or punishment depending upon the circumstances.

To weaken an undesirable behavior, you should think first of what behavior the student should be doing instead. This should bring to mind a desirable behavior which is incompatible with the expression of the undesirable behavior (they both cannot be exhibited at the same time). For example, a student cannot remain seated and run around the room at the same time, or he cannot be working on an assignment at the same time he is punching the student next to him. Your task is then to reward the expression of the desired alternative response as much as possible, while actively seeking to weaken the undesired one when it occurs.

Non-reinforcement is one technique which can be used effectively with undesirable behaviors which are relatively minor or infrequent or are not really disruptive or harmful to others (yelling out, goofy sounds, weird faces, complaining, tantrums, refusal to work). Non-reinforcement literally means the withholding of rewards. Research has shown that behaviors which are not reinforced tend to extinguish. In the context of the token economy, you can withhold reinforcement by not giving tokens to students and by physically ignoring them when they are engaging in the undesired behaviors. When you distribute tokens to the group, you must skip over a student who has failed to perform the specified behavior. The student will soon notice this and may begin to perform the appropriate response in anticipation of the next token. You can also withhold verbal and non-verbal attention to the student when he is engaging in an undesirable behavior. If you provide attention, pleasant or unpleasant, at the moment the behavior is occurring, you are likely to reinforce it, which you wish to avoid.

For behaviors which cannot be ignored because they are too disruptive, too persistent, or too threatening, you should structure an aversive (unpleasant) event following the behavior. When doing this, you should adhere, as much as possible, to the principle of negative reinforcement rather than punishment. Negative reinforcement differs from punishment in that its goal is the strengthening of a desirable alternative behavior and not just the suppression of an undesirable behavior. To accomplish this, the student must be informed of the appropriate behavior which will remove the aversive consequence. With punishment, however, the teacher does not give the student an "escape route" and merely expects the student not to misbehave again. As a result, punishment usually leads to only the temporary cessation of an undesirable behavior, with the response often "cropping up" as soon as the punishment is lifted.

Sometimes circumstances do not allow a teacher to make such fine distinctions between negative reinforcement and punishment, but the token economy system does offer a better framework to use aversive consequences to strengthen as well as weaken behavior. By utilizing a systematic, immediate, and "unemotional" set of consequences for undesirable behavior, the teacher can avoid becoming a tyrant, a victim, or an ex-teacher. By establishing clear procedures, the teacher in not forced to fall back on the typical cycle of nagging, threatening, yelling, and pleading.

In the model token economy, the major aversive consequence is "time out." With this technique, the student is removed (not by physical means, except in extraordinary circumstances) to a designated area immediately after an undesirable behavior occurs. The whole idea is that it is unpleasant to be taken away from the area where the student can enjoy the fruits of positive reinforcement, and, instead, be placed in a non-stimulating, unrewarding environment. The student is removed from the class activity so that he cannot interfere with other students and cannot obtain positive reinforcement (peer approval or teacher attention) for acting out. When the student commits himself to changing behavior to the desired alternative, or when he actually makes the change, or when he completes the time required, the student is returned to the class activity and resumes earning tokens.

Usually the "time out" area is located in an adjacent room, or if unavailable, a portion of the class area can be screened by positioning cabinets or partitions in a four-walled arrangement. The "time out" area should *not* be enclosed like a box and should not be made lockable, uncomfortable, dark, or frightening. It should simply be devoid of stimulation and potential reward. If the area is located inconspicuously, and away from the central activity, you will avoid some of the similarities to the "dunce in the corner."

To use "time out," you should first explain the procedures to the students and then insure that they are followed consistently and persistently. Immediately after a problem behavior occurs, the student should be walked over to the "time out." Later, when the procedure is well established, the student may be discreetly sent over to the area. You should ignore any verbal protestations and avoid arguing in any way. Reluctant learners are often experts at proclaiming their innocence and pinning blame on others, so attempts to "get to the bottom of things" are often futile. It is critical that you carry out this procedure dispassionately, so as not to create public displays of your anger or frustration (exciting stuff for onlookers).

Generally, you should approach the student when he is engaging in unacceptable behavior and simply say "time out." When the student arrives in the area, he should then be told exactly why he is there and how long he must stay, or what he must do to be allowed to return. To be consistent with the principle of negative reinforcement, the student should be permitted to return as soon as he engages in the desired alternative or makes a commitment to do so. When this is not possible or appropriate, a short time limit (5-25 minutes) should be set. This constitutes punishment more than negative reinforcement, but it can be effective when the desired alternative behaviors are already being reinforced by tokens in the class setting. Time periods should not be excessive (usually no more than 45 minutes) or else you run the risk of creating "time out" martyrs. Depending on the capacities of your students, you might allow them to release themselves from "time out" when the time period elapses or their behavior changes.

If a student refuses to go to "time out" or causes a disruption about it, he should be immediately escorted to the disciplinary administrator for possible suspension (if that is not in itself rewarding), or for parental conference, or for further isolation in the building. By reserving your most severe consequences for students who refuse to cooperate with "time out," rather than for the usual range of misbehaviors, you are likely to maintain the viability of the technique, and will be better able to take care of most undesirable behaviors within your class. The consequences for refusal should be made clear to students in advance.

It is essential that all teachers involved in the program use the technique in the same way and for the same behaviors, or else it will quickly lose its potency. It is usually a good idea to inform the students about the behaviors that will lead to "time out." These should be stated in general terms, since too much specificity may subject you to challenges by students who contend unfair treatment. In the model program, the following general behaviors are "time out" offenses:

1. Physical abuse (poking, hitting, tripping, pulling, pushing, etc.)

2. Verbal abuse of students or teachers.
3. Outright refusal to work.
4. Persistent acting out in class (calling out, throwing things, running around).

One note of caution here. The use of "time out," although extremely effective for most students of late elementary to early high school age, can be a problem if used with a large number of very rough students. Sometimes, especially when the numbers are on their side, such students can make a mockery of the procedure. If this is the case, the technique is likely to cause too much provocation and inadvertent reward, and it should not be used.

As part of your program, you might wish to include other, less dramatic aversive consequences. The key to their use, as with "time out," is planning. It must be clear to everyone in advance how and when you will employ the various techniques. In the model program the following techniques are employed: warning cues, private talks, and fines.

A warning cue is simply a verbal or non-verbal signal to the students telling them that if an undesirable behavior recurs, an aversive event will follow ("time out"). Where possible, you should use non-verbal warnings, like handing the student a red card or giving a hand signal, to avoid drawing attention to the student. If you warn verbally, it should be done quickly and personally, away from the attention of others. As a rule, warnings, regardless of their form, should be used only sparingly and for infrequently occurring behaviors. You do not want your cues to be so commonplace that the students become inured to them. You should also not use a series or hierarchy of warnings, because the students will soon discover that the first warning or two really means that there are further opportunities to misbehave before the "boom" actually falls. A teacher who warns excessively is one who inevitably ends up on a discipline escalator.

Private talks with students can sometimes be a useful way to change behavior. They usually work best with students who are basically reasonable to begin with and who have the self-control to change their behavior when consequences and implications are explained. If possible, these talks should be conducted away from view of other students, to avoid a spectacle. Also the talk should be conducted in a matter-of-fact manner, so the student does not think he is "getting your goat." You should simply express your disapproval of the undesirable behavior and specify the behavior you expect. You should generally permit the student to state his case, and then, without arguing, you should repeat your expectation modified in light of the student's comments. The student should then be returned to the class activity so that he has an immediate opportunity to demonstrate change and receive reward for doing so. If these talks become a pattern for a particular student, they should be dropped. This will be an indication that they are providing too much inadvertent reward for acting out.

Another way to weaken undesirable behavior is to withdraw rewards. The withdrawal of rewards is an easy and age-old method of punishing, but it should be generally avoided in a token economy system. It is usually more effective to withhold rewards in the first place, until they are properly earned, than to give them away and then snatch them back again. In the token economy, once a student has earned a back-up reward it must not be taken back, unless the student uses it in some forbidden manner. If a teacher withdraws an item or activity which the student has purchased with his tokens, the integrity of the system is undermined and the student unnecessarily provoked (as well we might be if someone withdrew something we purchased).

If anything is to be withdrawn under the system, it should be the tokens themselves. By withdrawing in this manner, you are, in effect, imposing a fine on the student for undesirable behavior. Fines can be effective in certain circumstances, but, as with warnings, they should be used only sparingly so that the system does not take on an excessively negative tone and the rewards lose their appeal. To help avoid this, tokens in hand should not be physically taken away when a fine is imposed. In other words, the teacher should not scratch off points or remove chips from the student's desk. Instead, the teacher should immediately record the assessed number of tokens on the student's bank record as points spent.

Fines are usually most effective when the withholding of tokens is not costly enough or does not lead to an alternative behavior. The problem behavior itself may actually be somewhat trivial but it may need quick resolution. For instance, if a student attempts to begin class without a pencil (after an initial opportunity to purchase one), he may stand to lose only one point for being unprepared. This does not produce a pencil and may be a small price to pay for an excuse not to work. By charging the student twice the token store price for a pencil, and requiring its immediate purchase, as well as withholding first point, you will probably solve the problem. Another way fines might be useful would be to assess them for each "time out." This may reduce the need for "time out," but it may also cause more negative reaction than it is worth.

Token Exchange Procedures

For both the chip economy and point economy, a banking system can be readily established, with the complexity of its structure based on the age and level of the students involved. A banking system not only permits an orderly procedure for exchanging tokens but it serves as an educational tool to teach basic concepts of earning, saving, and spending, which, in turn, provides a means to make math lessons more interesting and relevant. Depending on the sophistication of your overall token system, you might consider modeling your banking structure after actual methods used in banks, such as establishing checking accounts, paying interest and possibly even offering loans (although this should be handled very carefully).

The mechanics of a basic token banking system are really quite simple. At the end of each class day, your students count their earnings (chips or points) and record the total on their bank record. Figure 4, 5, and 6 provide examples of bank records (two for points and one for chips) with accompanying explanations, which have been used with middle school students. In designing any bank record, you should try to find a clear way to distinguish between what is earned, spent, and saved (with a running balance); many students find this quite confusing at first and need to have a good graphic arrangement to work with.

After the students record all of their daily transactions, they return the bank records to their designated storage place (file cabinet, desk, table, etc.) and turn in their chips (students do not leave the class with any chips in hand) or their point sheets (these must stay in the area as well, to prevent loss). One way to minimize confusion during the record-keeping time periods, especially since the students are usually not earning tokens during this brief period (unless you specifically design such a procedure), is to select or elect certain students to serve as bankers. You might even have the position be an earned privilege, which pays off with additional bonus points. The banker's duties can range from tallying the records of a small group at their table, or in their area, to gathering and distributing the records to and from their designated storage places. Whatever the duties, they should be carefully specified to avoid confusion and conflict over tasks.

For the point economy, you will need a time period at the beginning of class time to enable the students to secure their point sheet and bank record (if you wish them to carry it). You will also have to set aside time in the beginning of class under a chip economy (even though there is no sheet to pick up), if you are going to allow the students to make purchases to start the day (which must be recorded on the bank record). You will also have to provide a brief period of time at the end of class for students to tally their earnings and make purchases. These time periods might be utilized for other homebase purposes—making announcements, handing out papers, reconciling bank record mistakes, among other activities.

With the banking forms designed, you can now work out the mechanics of how the students can go about spending their earnings. To spend tokens, the students should be required to record the number to be spent in the appropriate column or box on their bank record.

The students should then fill out a coupon, noting their names, the number of tokens to be spent, and the date. They must then bring the coupons and their bank records to the teacher for verification. The teacher checks the savings balance for accuracy, initials the amount in the spend column, and signs the coupon. With the coupon in hand students may proceed to the store, activity, or lounge.

Evaluation Methods

One of the most commonly advocated methods for evaluating changes in student behavior under a token system is the comparison of baselines which have been taken before and after the intervention of the system. There is no doubt that this technique, as described in Figure 1, can generate very specific and helpful information, but, unfortunately, it has limited application. As may be obvious, baselining is not terribly practical for measuring behavior changes in each student in the class, despite what many behaviorists would argue. The technique is very time consuming and often re-requires an additional person to serve as the data collector. If such additional personnel are available, baselining should be chosen as the main evaluative tool; but, if not, then other methods will probably have to be employed.

One major alternative for measuring change in an individual's behavior, although admittedly less precise, is to make comparisons of administrative records before and after the student's involvement in the program. You might compare attendance figures, disciplinary referrals, parent contacts, or other "front office" data. This could then be coupled with the teacher's personal, and hopefully objective, assessments of specified behavior before and after intervention. These records will provide at least informal data on changes in a range of specific social behaviors.

For academic behaviors, there are many ways to assess achievement. In the basic skills, especially math and reading, there are numerous instruments which provide pre- and post-data on skill levels. It is probably a good idea to administer a standardized test before the students enter the program (if this is possible) to be compared with results on a parallel form after intervention of the program. No matter how much norm-referenced tests are criticized in the literature, educators and parents still demand, perhaps more than ever, this type of data. Fortunately, the research indicates that token systems are very effective in raising standardized test scores.

Criterion-referenced tests also have good uses in the token system. As with other evaluation techniques, each student can be measured before and after participation in the system to determine progress. Since mastery tests are now being widely adopted as a high school graduation requirement, it would be useful to include them in the system. In fact, some students may have to depend on involvement in a token economy or some other alternative program to ultimately help them to graduate.

The standard method for reporting progress in the schools is, of course, letter grades. The use of letter grades should certainly not be overlooked for inclusion in the system. If properly used, as they often are not, letter grades can be a useful and convenient way to symbolize performance levels. Besides, the school system or parents may demand that you use them. Parents often prefer grades to other reporting techniques, like conferences, which they find too threatening or too difficult to arrange. It is likely, however, that most of the students selected for a token program will have had miserable experiences with grades prior to entry into the program. Many will have given up by the time they reach you, and will probably subscribe to the theory that it is just as easy to fail to try than to fail trying. Therefore, you will have to give grades a new meaning and a new accessibility. Your method must insure that effort yields rewards and non-effort yields no rewards (but not necessarily punishment). It serves little purpose to give failing grades until students are prepared to expend effort and compete with themselves and others. Failing grades are too often given for purely punitive purposes ("to give the kid what he deserves"), and the results are generally negligible. Furthermore, this approach tends to play into the hands of reluctant learners, providing them with badges of honor for bucking the system.

By using tokens as the basis for assigning grades, you can avoid most of the traditional pitfalls. If you explain from the outset that the letter grades will be based on the accumulated tokens earned, the students are more likely to see them as incentives. Under this procedure, social and academic target behaviors can be combined in the evaluation process and reflected in the grades. These behaviors do not have to be combined, but it is often a good idea, since the students' social behavior is likely to have a direct impact on their ability to perform academic tasks. To be reinforcing, high grades must seem accessible to each student in the class. So in the beginning, at least, it might be best to put more emphasis on quantity than quality of work. This is important because many students have to be reinforced initially for just handing in work, even if only partially complete. Then, as the work product increases, the token criteria can be altered to require better quality as well. It is also probably not a good idea to give any letter grades before the end of the marking period. If you do, and the grades are skewed high to increase incentive, they may lose their potency from overexposure. On the other hand, if you attempt to give a full range of grades, from "A to E," along the way, you run the risk of unnecessarily frustating students who receive the poor marks.

Parent conferences and home visits are another commonly recommended reporting method which can be useful for the system, if handled properly. The conferences are usually most productive when they focus on specific behaviors, rather than vague discussions of student attitudes, and when they provide parents with suggested strategies for supporting target behaviors at home. It is often possible to provide useful hints about how to apply various reinforcement techniques at home. For instance, it is helpful to point out how a student might earn various privileges at home rather than having them merely handed out and then capriciously taken away for punishment. In other words, parents can support the school's work by rearranging reinforcement contingencies to require that each available reward be earned by demonstrating productive behaviors (perhaps related to school) instead of automatically granting them (unearned) and then revoking them because they are undeserved.

Some parent contacts should be made for the sole purpose of reporting only positive change. Parents of reluctant learners are often surprised and excited by phone calls or visits from school personnel which are pleasant and not laced with distressing news, as in the past. If their contacts with school are generally favorable, parents are more likely to be supportive of the program. The "Super Letter" shown in Figure 2 is one of the easiest methods for maintaining positive contact and keeping the parents informed of student progress.

To accompany grade reports or evaluation conferences, a behavior checklist might be devised. The checklist should include the target behaviors you are working on, stated in positive terms so as not to give the checklist an overwhelmingly negative tone. It should be worded so that it specifically informs the parent about the behaviors which have improved and which have not.

To measure the overall effectiveness of the program, you will need to return to the techniques you used in measuring individual behavior change. You can readily compare the group means of pre- and post-baselines of selected social behaviors. This is probably the most useful data you can obtain. You might also wish to compare the pre- and post-totals pertaining to attendance figures, suspensions, office referrals, parent contacts, and other administrative data on the group of students. A survey instrument might also be useful, if your students can handle it, for measuring before and after changes in the group's attitudes toward themselves and their academic progress. You will also probably want to compare the mean change in standardized test scores, and the mastery levels on criterion-references tests, to show the group's overall growth in achievement.

Summary

To insure good results with the token economy system,

each of the components above must be carefully worked out to fit the particular needs of your school. You should not attempt to involve students in the program until the organizational details are complete—the rewards selected, target behaviors specified, token procedures established, and evaluation methods determined. If the token economy is born in confusion and uncertainty, its initial potency and long-term effèctiveness will suffer severely, with the students falling back on familiar patterns of disruption and avoidance. It is essential, therefore, that the students sense from the first day that they are part of a unique and total experience which offers real opportunity for success and little pay-off for undesirable behaviors. This will require from the outset a learning atmosphere which is calm, orderly, businesslike, and, of course, reinforcing.

IV.

OUTCOMES

The major outcome you can expect from using a token economy system, when it is employed as an alternative program within the school, is that the participating students will learn to function more effectively in the school environment, while the learning atmosphere in the remainder of the school improves dramatically. The token system allows the school to carry out its daily business in a more orderly, interesting, and fruitful manner because the reluctant learners are temporarily removed from settings in which they interfere with the learning of others or in which they are unable or unwilling to do the work. In the system, these students are provided the type of structure they need and can relate to—a structure which sets clearly defined limits and offers a range of appealing rewards for productive behaviors.

If the system is designed properly, you should fully expect that a number of your students will obtain sufficient self-control and motivation to be able to return to the "regular" programs as the year progresses. The reintegration of the students should always remain a primary consideration for anyone running a token system. It must not become a stigmatizing experience or a "dead end" warehouse for dysfunctional students. One way to avoid this is to schedule the students into at least one or two classes per day with the general population outside the system. Another procedure, which should be carefully followed, is for the teachers in the system to meet every six to eight weeks to determine if any students are prepared to "graduate" from the program.

With these general statements in mind, it is now possible to state more specifically what you can expect from the token economy approach:

1. The token economy promotes positive change in a range of social and academic behaviors in students who have been reluctant to learn.

2. The system allows for the establishment of a more reinforcing environment than is generally possible in existing programs.

3. The system actively reinforces students for developing self-control of their social behavior and thus allows them to have more harmonious relationships.

4. As designed, the system actively shapes and maintains essential learning habits (listening to instructions, concentrating on tasks, bringing necessary materials) which are prerequisites for increased achievement.

5. Through the use of various rewards, not practical in other settings, the students are given a new motivation to learn.

6. With increased motivation, improved social interactions, and new learning habits, the students will substantially increase their achievement levels, especially in basic skill areas. Because the students are less disruptive or less withdrawn they can become more productive, and vice versa.

7. The system provides an organizational framework in which a variety of instructional strategies can be employed successfully. It allows different types of instruction to "take hold" because the students are orderly and ready to learn.

8. Since the system anticipates many of the typical discipline problems, the number of referrals to the office, suspensions, detentions, and parent contacts will decline signifi-

cantly. The token economy allows the school to break the pattern of constantly escalating or revolving-door punishments with the same group of students.

9. Because the program is reinforcing, and therefore more enjoyable to be part of, student attendance will improve markedly.

10. Although the program will certainly not guarantee that the participating students will function effectively in settings outside the system, it is likely to decrease the general vandalism, violence, and class cutting within the entire school. If the program is meaningful for the students (as has proved to be true with many hundreds of students), they will tend to be more committed to the school and less destructive.

11. As has been pointed out, the school as a whole is likely to become more orderly and productive as a consequence of the reluctant learners' involvement in the program. There will no longer be a "hard core" of students in each class whose behavior prohibits the other members from learning with maximum freedom.

12. The token economy system can also prove to be an extremely effective way to bring special education students into the "mainstream." When learning disabled, or retarded, or emotionally handicapped students are merely thrown into the "regular" mix, even with access to a resource teacher, the results are often poor. The students can become too easily frustrated and disoriented. The token economy, on the other hand, provides a more responsive structure for these students' common needs, especially in the early stages of reintegration. It also permits the school to concentrate all its specialized and support personnel in one program, instead of diffusing their efforts.

13. Having said all these favorable things about the expected outcomes of the token economy system (which are rooted entirely in practical experience), one serious limita-

tion should be explored. As has been pointed out, the students as a group will be highly productive and orderly while in the token system, if it has been run properly. The atmosphere will be calm and pleasant, with teachers rarely having to raise their voices and students rarely off task. Most students will clearly enjoy the experience, and, in fact, prefer it. But, do not expect the system to control all the behavior problems of the participating students when they are outside the reinforcement setting (in the halls, on the buses, in the cafeteria, and in other classes). Experience has shown that, while there can be good "carry over" with some students, it cannot be fairly stated that the program has effective transfer value for the group as a whole. Desirable behaviors are only relatively certain within the token arrangement, or after a student has "graduated." Knowing this, the individuals who establish a token system should be careful not to raise the expectations of those who work with students outside the reinforcement context.

V.

DEVELOPMENTAL GUIDE

By following the procedures below, as depicted also in Figure 7, you should be able to set up a complete token economy system in your school.

1.0 DETERMINE SCOPE OF PROBLEM
1.1 *Make Initial Observations*
Your task here is to look at what is actually happening in the existing school programs. The type of behaviors to be targeted and the dimensions of the problems they pose will determine if a token economy system is necessary.
1.2 *Decide If The Token System Is Really Needed*
If your analysis indicates that a change in curriculum or in the social reinforcers would resolve your problems, you will not, of course, need a token economy. If your problems seem localized to just a few students, you may also wish to pursue an alternative other than the token economy, although some of its components might prove useful in devising individual strategies.

If it appears that a sizeable group of students are not likely to respond to the changes suggested above, you should proceed to the next step.

Figure 7

Developmental Sequence

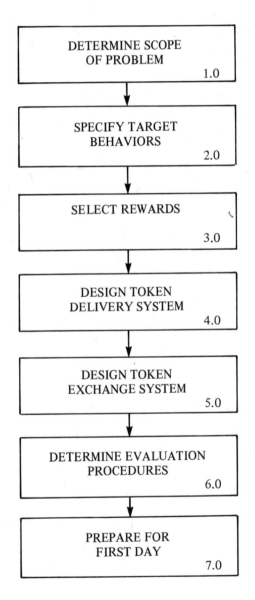

2.0 SPECIFY TARGET BEHAVIORS ·

2.1 *Baseline Student Social Behavior*

Using a technique like that described in Figure 1, you should gather data of undesirable behaviors among the students you intend to select for the program

2.2 *Assess Student Academic Behavior*

Review all recent test data on the students, go over the learning objectives in their classes, and then administer norm-referenced tests which will give an accurate picture of the student's entry levels.

2.3 *Compile A List Of Target Behaviors*

After gathering your data, you should isolate the major behaviors you wish the students to perform in the program. In specific terms, you will be stating the behaviors they need to learn in order to function more effectively in the school.

2.4 *Establish Objectives*

Here you will be specifying the terminal behaviors you expect the students to be able to perform before leaving the program. These should include the social behaviors and academic skills which are most realistic.

3.0 SELECT REWARDS

3.1 *Determine The Type Of Token*

The type of token you choose will depend on the size of your group, the students' ages and level of sophistication, and the length of your involvement with the students each day (number of subjects per day).

3.2 *Compile A List Of Potential Rewards*

You should brainstorm with all the staff to be

involved in the program to determine the types of back-up rewards you intend to offer. It is helpful to think of the various categories of rewards: material items, activities, privileges, awards, grades, edibles.

3.3 *Compute Your Budget*

Before you go any further, you will need to know how much money you have available for purchasing the various rewards. You may need to explore a number of funding sources: school funds, private contributions, government funding, etc.

3.4 *Prepare For Student Input*

It is a good idea to actively involve the students in selecting the actual rewards to be used. Their choices should be solicited on the first day of the program, and at various intervals through the year.

3.5 *Schedule Reward Activities*

You will need to determine how and when the honors meetings ("Super Letters" and awards) and auctions will be held, along with other activities which are to occur regularly during the year.

4.0 DESIGN TOKEN DELIVERY SYSTEM

4.1 *Plan Overall Strategies Of Reinforcement*

Before considering the mechanics of distributing tokens, you should study about reinforcement principles and determine how positive, negative, and non-reinforcement will be generally applied in your program. Particular emphasis should be placed on how social reinforcers will be used in a systematic and generous fashion. You should also decide if "time out" is to be used and for what offenses.

4.2 *Determine Distribution Method*

Here you will have to decide on the most efficient and effective way to distribute the type of
token you have chosen. If a point sheet is needed,
you will have to work out its basic design, which
will depend, of course, on the number of academic
subjects to be taken by the students. See Figures 3
and 5 for two point sheet models.

4.3 *Set Token Schedules For The Target Behaviors*

You should now establish the relative token
value of each target behavior and the schedule of
reinforcement for it. You will need to consider
which behaviors should be under a fixed or variable
ratio, and which should be under fixed or variable
interval. At this time, you should also determine
the token values of work output and decide how to
relate the tokens to grades.

5.0 DESIGN TOKEN EXCHANGE SYSTEM

5.1 *Determine Banking Procedures*

First you will need to design the bank record itself, which will depend upon the type of
token and the overall complexity of the system.
See Figures 4, 5, and 6 for bank record models.
You will then have to decide how the banking
procedures can actually be scheduled into the class
sessions.

5.2 *Determine Spending Procedures*

You need to decide here how the coupons will
be used in your system and how the store and
lounge will operate.

5.3 *Set Price Of Rewards*

At this point, you should attempt to establish
the initial prices of all the reward items and ac-

tivities, including how the students can qualify for privileges and awards.

6.0   DETERMINE EVALUATION PROCEDURES

6.1   *Select Methods For Measuring Student Progress*

Here you will need to decide upon your methods for measuring changes in the students' social and academic behavior. For social behavior, you can compare baselines (taken before and after intervention of the system), or administrative data, or teacher records. For academic behaviors you have a variety of norm-referenced and criterion-referenced tests to choose from.

6.2   *Select Methods For Reporting Student Performance*

The most obvious reporting tool is, of course, grades, which, if handled in a reinforcing way, can be effective under the system. You can also arrange parent contacts to discuss behavior change strategies and to give positive feedback. Checklists can be sent home to show the specific behaviors being worked on. Letters should also be sent home frequently indicating student progress.

6.3   *Select Methods For Measuring Program Effectiveness*

Here you are concerned with gathering group data. Baselines can provide the most specific information about overall changes in social behavior. The data found in administrative records, on such things as suspensions, referrals, and attendance may be helpful in comparing the groups' behavior before and after involvement in the program. You might also have the teachers record their own observations of specified social behavior before and after intervention. It might be interesting to include an attitude survey with the students to assess their own feelings about involvement in the program. For academic behaviors, the data drawn from pre- and post-testing with norm-referenced and criterion-referenced instruments will be most instructive.

7.0 PREPARE FOR FIRST DAY

7.1 *Organize The Physical Environment*

You will need to locate sufficient space within the school to conduct the program. Then you will have to carefully arrange the furniture and the token centers (lounge, store, etc.) to minimize interference.

7.2 *Specify Instructional And Operational Responsibilities*

Before the program actually begins, you will need to be sure that each staff member knows his functions. The assignment for preparing lessons and dispensing rewards should be clearly established. If you are working on your own, then you will need to work out how to instruct and reward at the same time.

7.3 *Practice Reinforcement Procedures*

All persons involved in the program should go through the paces of distributing tokens, ignoring minor distractions, using "time out," and, most importantly, supplying generous helpings of social reinforcers for the students.

7.4 *Plan Program Orientation For Students*

You will need to work out how and when you will explain the program to the students involved. See Figure 8 for an agenda of such a meeting.

7.5 *Recheck Program Details*

Before the first day, you should make certain you have accounted for all the ingredients of the system. It is critical that the program start off in a highly organized manner. See Figure 9 for a program checklist.

Figure 8

Agenda for First Day

I. **Briefly introduce the idea of the token system**
    A. Use of points or chips for good behavior
    B. Purchase of rewards (store, auctions, activities, privileges)
    C. Start using tokens

II. **Specify how rewards can be earned**
    A. Post and discuss list of rules (you might call them "Positive Behaviors")
    B. Describe how the tokens will be distributed

III. **Discuss the rewards**
    A. *The store*
        1. give tentative list of material items
        2. describe procedure for use
        3. solicit student suggestions
    B. *The lounge*
        1. list available activities
        2. describe procedure for use
        3. solicit student suggestions
    C. *Auctions*
        1. list proposed items
        2. describe procedure
        3. solicit student suggestions
    D. *Activities*
        1. list trips and other available events
        2. describe procedure
        3. solicit student suggestions
    E. *Privileges*
        1. list special jobs (roll runner, storekeepers, bankers, media operator, etc.)
        2. describe procedure
        3. solicit student suggestions
    F. *Honors*
        1. discuss use of "Super Letters," certificates, and trophies
        2. describe procedure
        3. solicit student suggestions

(Continued on next page)

Figure 8 (Continued)

IV. **Demonstrate banking procedures (use overhead projector or chalkboard)**
    A.   Hand out record samples
    B.   Describe record-keeping process
V. **Explain the evaluation methods**
    A.   Discuss how performance will be measured and reported
    B.   Describe how the tokens are involved
    C.   Demonstrate how the record will be kept
VI. **Explain use of "time out"**
    A.   Main method for dealing with unacceptable behavior
    B.   List offenses
    C.   Discuss how yelling, threatening, and warning will not be used much to deal with bad behavior
    D.   Describe "time out" procedure
VII. **Simulate the token system**
    A.   Give a practice assignment
    B.   Distribute tokens
    C.   Practice banking
    D.   Give bonus tokens for good cooperation with these procedures

Figure 9

Program Checklist

Purchase Token Materials
. . . .tokens, carpenter nail belt
. . . .felt pens
. . . .folders and notebooks
. . . .reward items for store, lounge, auction, breaks

Prepare Token Materials
. . . .reproduce all records (point sheets, bank records)
. . . .write out "Super Letter" and reproduce
. . . .design achievement certificate
. . . .design and reproduce store coupon
. . . .print up rules
. . . .print up price list
. . . .print up reward list
. . . .print up lounge rules

Organize Token Centers
. . . .arrange record filing areas (file cabinets, desks, etc.)
. . . .set up and stock lounge
. . . .set up (in lockable cabinet) and stock store
. . . .set up "time out" area
. . . .arrange materials for breaks

Organize Class Area
. . . .arrange desks and tables
. . . .arrange instructional materials
. . . .locate media equipment

Complete Instructional Preparations
. . . .lessons for first days
. . . .back-up activities and work sheets
. . . .pre-tests and diagnostic instruments
. . . .assign student groups
. . . .determine daily class schedule
. . . .agenda for first day with students

(Continued on next page)

Figure 9 (Continued)

Review Duties and Procedures
. . . .distribute list of duties and procedures to each teacher-operator
. . . .rehearse aides on techniques

Miscellaneous
. . . .assign student seats
. . . .prepare bathroom passes

VI.

RESOURCES

In recent years token economy systems have had wide applicaton in the fields of education, mental health, and corrections. Exhaustive research literature is now available on the various designs which have been employed. Generally, however, these programs have been used with small samples of students, or in atypical educational settings, or with highly specialized personnel. This program, on the other hand, has been used with large groups of students, in typical school settings, with regular teachers. For these reasons, this design is somewhat unique.

BOOKS

A. To obtain a theoretical background in reinforcement principles, you may wish to consult:

Bandura, A. *Principles of Behavior Modification.* New York: Holt, Rinehart, and Winston, 1969.

Keller, F. S. *Learning: Reinforcement Theory.* New York: Random House, 1968.

Skinner, B. F. *Contingencies of Reinforcement: A Theoretical Analysis.* New York: Appleton-Century-Crofts, 1969.

B. If you wish to consider the philosophical implications of behavior reinforcement, you may enjoy:

Skinner, B. F. *Beyond Freedom and Dignity.* New
York: Alfred A. Knopf, 1971.

Skinner, B. F. *About Behaviorism.* New York: Alfred
A. Knopf, 1974.

C. For easier discussions of reinforcement principles and
for their applications to the school, the following will
be helpful:

Buckley, N. K., and H. M. Walker. *Modifying Classroom Behavior.* Champaign, Illinois: Research
Press, 1970.

Clarizio, H. F. *Toward Positive Classroom Discipline.*
New York: John Wiley and Sons, 1971.

Krumboltz, J. D., and C. E. Thoresen. *Behavioral
Counseling.* New York: Holt, Rinehart and Win-
stone, 1969.

Madsen, C. H., and C. K. Madsen. *Teaching/Discipline
Behavioral Principles: Toward a Positive Approach.*
Boston: Allyn and Bacon, 1970.

Meacham, M. L., and A. E. Wiesen. *Changing Classroom Behavior.* Scranton, Pennsylvania: International Textbook Co., 1971.

D. For staff training, the following will be useful:

Martin, R., and D. Lauridsen. *Developing Student Motivation and Discipline: A Series for In-Service
Training.* Champaign, Illinois: Research Press,
1974.

E. Two books which will provide additional ideas for
setting up a token economy system are:

Walker, H. M., and N. K. Buckley. *Token Reinforcement Procedures.* Eugene, Oregon: E-B Press,
1974.

Stainback, W. C., J. S. Payne, S. A. Stainback, and
R. A. Payne. *Establishing a Token Economy in*

the Classroom. Columbus, Ohio: Charles E. Merrill, 1973.

F. To involve parents in the reinforcement process, this pamphlet will be helpful:

Alvord, J.R. *Home Token Economy.* Champaign, Illinois: Research Press, 1973.

G. If you are involved in setting up a program outside the regular school, or in using a token economy system for experimental purposes, you should be aware of the ethical and legal considerations discussed in:

Martin, R. *Legal Challenges to Behavior Modification.* Champaign, Illinois: Research Press, 1975.

FILMS

For a fairly complete picture of the workings of this particular token economy system in the regular school setting, you should secure:

Education of Disruptive Students
Film Production Service
Virginia Department of Education
Richmond, Virginia 23216

For a token economy operating in an alternative school setting, see:

The ABC's of Behavioral Education
Hallmark Films
1511 E. North Avenue
Baltimore, Maryland 21213

WORKSHOPS AND CONSULTING
The author conducts workshops on the use of general behavior modification techniques in schools and serves as a consultant for schools wishing to establish a token economy system.

DAVID LAURIDSEN is presently a counselor/teacher at Hammond Middle School in Laurel, Maryland, where he oversees the token economy program he has designed. During his nine years in secondary schools, Mr. Lauridsen has been primarily concerned with devising behavioral strategies to help troubled students, a topic on which he has published before. He now frequently consults with schools wishing to adopt his approaches, and has conducted numerous workshops on behavior modification techniques for parents and teachers. While completing his Ph.D. at the University of Maryland, Mr. Lauridsen is also serving as a part-time instructor in secondary education methods and classroom management.